Earthsleep

Also by Fred Chappell

The World Between the Eyes

It Is Time, Lord

The Inkling

Dagon

The Gaudy Place

River

Bloodfire

Wind Mountain

Moments of Light

LOUISIANA STATE UNIVERSITY PRESS

Earthsleep A Poem

Fred Chappell

BATON ROUGE AND LONDON   1980

Parts of this poem first appeared in *Arts Journal*,
Epoch, Georgia Review, Hollow Spring Review, The Lyricist,
Quarterly West, and *Texas Review*.

LIBRARY OF CONGRESS CATALOGING IN PUBLICATION DATA

Chappell, Fred, 1936–
  Earthsleep.

  I.   Title.
PS3553.H298E3   811'.54   80–13622
ISBN 0–8071–0697–6
ISBN 0–8071–0698–4 (pbk.)

The author wishes to dedicate this book to the memory of his father, Mr. J. T. Chappell.

He wishes also to acknowledge Logan's Bar in Greensboro, N.C., for many kindnesses aiding in composition.

Now comes the peal of the distant clock, with fainter and fainter strokes as you plunge farther into the wilderness of sleep. It is the knell of a temporary death. Your spirit has departed, and strays, like a free citizen, among the people of a shadowy world, beholding strange sights, yet without wonder or dismay. So calm, perhaps, will be the final change; so undisturbed, as if among familiar things the entrance of the soul to its Eternal home!

—Hawthorne

Contents

Earthsleep

Earth Emergent Drifts the Fire River

Shoves us landward, straining and warping like kites.

Yellow ring of earth bobs up to eye-level
At the blowing window.
                    The cool deep morning
Begins to fashion the trees, flesh-tree
And tree of spirit, haranguing the land with birds.

                              Sleep, love, keep
Still.
Why would you ever wake?
My mind in your blood discovers each dream of earth
And every earth. Mind coming apart to blood, windblown
Islands of fire voyage that headlong ocean your blood,
Blood's-breath warms and swells the bedroom,
Room where sleep takes its monstrous earthshape, room where
My thirty-fifth birthday, 28 May 1971, waits
To devour my bit of flesh,
My bit of fire.

Terrible to know this day raising over houses its wind,
Wind of change no real change,
Fire colors the military maps, each village a red coal,
Water leached through sand leaves
Not the vaguest map-shape, history
Too thirsty, bloodthirsty; and earth
Adrift in wind.
The birdsong tiers of my dream are the screams
Of the immolated and the self-immolated.
And the drowned men swim unbearably toward us.

                         The window is raucous with sunlight,
Water-warble, daybreeze, the window
Opens into the furnace of spirit, the cranky

Obbligato of bluejay, stinksparrow, opens the flames of morning.
The cool contralto mourning dove
Is the one clear note of soothe in the world
Going up in flame. *The furious net*
Of daylight plumbs the bed. We are, Susan, lifted
Dripping with sparkle toward the earliest sun.
In dayfire the trees lose their forms, green leaves
Glow like knifeblades, the waters down
Among the dead rob the birds of song, light
Strips world-shape to half-dream, it is the
Windy delirium of fire, the Silver Planet is taking our
World of warm wet, I do not wish to be
Consumed by spirit merely, I do not wish
To be consumed. I do not
Wish to be. I do
Not wish.

        An ecstasy of forgetting
And aspiring. What there is in emptiness,
What limits, what foreknowledge, what improbable coldness, what
Hatred for the spirit-tree, the tree of flesh,
What there is, let it consume itself,
Let it mass and flounder yonder from the skin
Of things, let it not come nigh this hearth, this hold,
This house, let the cloud of unbeing never touch
Our garish boxes of fervor. Susan, we must dream
The sinewy dream, the dream militant,
We must thrust at bay all that is dreamless.
Here are we perched unsteady on the margin of dream,
Receiving from two worlds their gaudy intelligence.
World of half-sleep,
World of waking,
              where the four-square crucis of elements
Cuts clean across. Yet are we
Given to know beyond these Another,
                  where no water sings with
Its breath of fire, where sunlight the cloud never

Ripens to peach, where the single atoms stray
Lost and touchless, where even the longdrawn shriek
Of history sounds a thin sigh merely, it is
That world we send our fireships to destroy.
Not death, no, there is no
Death, only a deeper dreaming. But there is
                    Nothing,
The black egg seedless hatching its harsh wings.
Yet is Whitman not delivered to it, nor Thoreau.
Nor the human deaths of lovers,
It cannot gorge them.

                    I push more fiercely
My face to your breast, my forehead suckles your shoulder.
Do I not hear in you patches of light
Like the little gold-red marigolds chirping at sunset?
Peeling of sun-skin like the handshaped poplar leaves
Spinning down in first October? Gleams of coins
Of watershine in the white slant dawn?
I hear clearly this jazz of piecemeal light,
Glitter on glitter of melodic line
Atop its dense profound harmony of shadow.
                              Rattle and thump,
The drumming of sun on the river, what fun,
And that trumpet passage where sunstreak
Goes from treecrown to treecrown like a card trick,
That's the streaming, sun/slice   light/dark   sun/slice,
Of light through the boarded barn. Light is sound,
We hear it in the trees at daybreak.

Falling towers of lace
And spittle:
                the light in the trees
At daybreak, filigree of sugar icing, it is
A wedding cake, no, it is a highly fanciful birthday cake,
Hullo ole Fred Welcome to Life and Death,
1st day my 35th year the world.
Sun/slice   off/on   dark/light   death/life   dark/light.

These waters crept to me
Within the music: sand-thrilled spring water,
The tepid slackwater of West Fork Pigeon River,
Baptismal water, perfume of tongue-and-groove pine,
Steaming lakewater at daybreak. I stroke
The water upward, waking, I
Am rising, I dream no more drowning,
I leap toward the surface, bubbles of breath
Surround my eyes, little worlds in water, spheres
Of perfect music, I shall escape from drowning
Into a world of waters, my grandmother's feet in water
The dreambloated roots of cypress,
Death-well where noon sun is caught,
Water that bears away the whiskey earth, I
Am dreaming these no more, I am content,
Susan, to see you step forward from the drizzle,
Ideal taking form in history, touchpoint of
Vision and blood, your pinkened foot on cool tile,
Here is your towel, rough terry cleanses the
Word of life, you are the spirit of water
By sweet fire tempered to earth, speak you,
Tell me some elder annunciation, tell me
History is being reborn in water, in healing water
Rise all the cities gone down, the nations who
Died in the fire of blood take clean new bodies,
A silver ivy of water reclaims the broken walls,
Unguessed Atlantises poke their streaming heads
Out of the history books, sins of the fathers
To lordly earth overgiven rise
Again now transformed to the great names we feed upon,
The fertile waters of deathsleep manure the flames.

"What now can be said of air?"
The small breathing of earth, souls aswoon in wind,
Wind is the suffering of spirit, unfocused
Directionless desire, here driven and there in space
We are unhoused, unhouseled,

Wind Mountain pours its cold poverty on the land,
Searches the man rock-wedged, searches his flesh
Every vulnerable nook of it, his soul
Tatters in barren rocktooth wind,
He dies except he lives, lives exalted
As the burly Spirit uplifts his spirit amid
What poor stones, I go to the mountain
To be upraised humble, on the mountain we spread our
Picnic blanket, my grandfather's evanished church sighs
In the wind, this is the melancholy of never forgetting,
The bones in air, music music of
Expectant freedom, I do desire you now.

Susan, we are gone we have come
To earth.
The resplendent house of spirit bursts around the body.
Mind rises from the ravages of sense
And clothes in dream. Mind, old Crusoe,
Are you here lost with me on this island of fire,
This bright and lonely spark struck off
In the heave of bloodsea?
Earth, where do you take us, will you
Shed us upon the black waters streaming
Deathward?
Will you deliver us to wind,
In wind to suffer shorn of flesh, crying
Our mewling cry?
Or thrust us
Into the fire, into the raging ecstasy
Of purified spirit, of burning foreknowledge?

                                       Do not us Earth
Remember.
                  Leave us, mud jumble of mirk
And humus, tucked in the rock heart
Of the mountain, in these stones are seeds of fire,
Dream-seeds which taking root shall renew the world,
Tree of Spirit lifting from the mountain of earth

As the curtains of fire rise behind our eyelids,
Spirit Tree of Fire overglowing all the world,
Seeking with its flower-light
Each crinkle in the rock, each crease
In the dark heart hid from the head.

I feel your touch, Earthflesh,
Here my birthday is.

Birthday 35, 28 May 1971.

                        Okay,
I gird myself.
I'll wear my clothes, my naked clothes.

> *Rock me gently, gentle Earth,*
> *In air, in fire, in water, I am steeped.*
> *And every promise I shall keep*
> *That I have promised while I slept.*

Hello Destiny, I'm harmless Fred,
Treat me sweet Please.

My Mother's Hard Row to Hoe

Hard, I say. Mostly I can't think how
To make it clear, the times have changed so much.
Maybe it's not possible to know
Now how we lived back then, it was such
A different life.
                                    "Did you like it?"
                                                                    I
Felt that I had to get away or die
Trying. I felt it wasn't *me* from dawn
To dawn, "slaving my fingers to the bone,"
As Mother used to say; and yet so bored
It was a numbing torture to carry on.
Because that world was just plain hard.

Mother was always up at five o'clock,
Winter and summer, and jarred us out of bed
With her clanging milkcans and the knock
Of water in the pipes. Out to the shed
I went, and milked five cows and poured the milk
Into the cans—so rich it looked like silk

And smelled like fresh-cut grass. Then after that
The proper work-day started. I did what
She told me to, no never-mind how tired
I was, and never once did she run out,
Because that world was just plain hard.

Because from May through August we put up hay
And worked tobacco and, sure as you were born,
We'd find the hottest stillest July day
To start off in the bottom hoeing corn.
From the pear orchard to the creek's big bend,
Corn rows so long you couldn't see the end;

And never a breeze sprang up, never a breath
Of fresh, but all as still and close as death.
We hoed till dark. I was hoeing toward
A plan that would preserve my mental health,
Because that world was so almighty hard.

I'd get myself more schooling, and I'd quit
These fields forever where the hoe clanged stone
Wherever you struck, and the smell of chickenshit
Stayed always with you just like it was your own.
I felt I wasn't *me*, but some hired hand
Who was being underpaid to work the land,
Or maybe just a fancy farm machine
That had no soul and barely a jot of brain
And no more feelings than any cat in the yard
And not good sense to come out of the rain.
That world, I say, was just too grinding hard.

But I'd learn Latin and Spanish and French and math
And English literature. Geography.
I wouldn't care if I learned myself to death
At the University in Tennessee
So long as I could tell those fields goodbye
Forever, for good and all and finally.
—"You really hated it then?"
                                    No, that's not true.
. . . Well, maybe I did. It's hard to know
Just how you feel about a place; a blurred
Mist-memory comes over it all blue,
No matter if that place was flintrock hard.

There were some things I liked, of course there were:
I walked out in the morning with the air
All sweet and clean and promiseful and heard
A mourning dove—. . . *No! I couldn't care.*
You've got to understand how it was *hard*.

My Father Washes His Hands

I pumped the iron handle and watched the water
Cough his knuckles clean. Still he kept rubbing,
Left hand in his right like hefting a baseball;
The freckles might have scaled off with the clay.
But didn't. They too were clay, he said, that mud
The best part maybe of apparent spirit.

"What spirit?" I asked.
                        He grinned and got the soap
Again and sloshed. A bubble moment I saw
Our two faces little in his palm.
"The Spirit of Farming," he said, "or the Soul of Damnfool."
Our faces went away and showed his lifeline.
"Damnfool why?"
                    "A man's a fool in this age
Of money to turn the soil. Never a dime
To call his own, and wearing himself away
Like a kid's pencil eraser on a math lesson.
I've got a mind to quit these fields and sell
Cheap furniture to poor folks. I've got a mind
Not to die in the traces like poor Honey."
(Our jenny mule had died two weeks before.)
"A man's not the same as a mule," I said.

He said, "You're right. A man doesn't have the heart . . .
We buried Honey, me and Uncle Joe,
While you were away at school. I didn't tell you.
Two feet down we hit pipe clay as blue
And sticky as Buick paint. Octopus-rassling,
Uncle Joe called it. Spade would go down
Maybe two inches with my whole weight behind
And come up empty. Blue glue with a spoon.
I soon decided to scale down the grave.

I told him straight, *I'm going to bust her legs*
And fold them under. His face flashed red at once.
My God, J.T., poor Honey that's worked these fields
For thirteen years, you'd bust her legs? I nodded.
She can't feel a thing, I said. He says,
By God I do. I told him to stand behind
The truck and stop his ears. I busted her legs.
I busted her legs with the mattock, her eyes all open
And watching me crack her bones and bulging out
Farther slightly with every blow. These fields
Were in her eyes, and a picture of me against
The sky blood-raw savage with my mattock.
I leaned and thumbed her eye shut and it was like
Closing a book on an unsatisfactory
Last chapter not pathetic and not tragic,
But angrifying mortifying sad.
The harder down I dug the bluer I got,
And empty as my shovel. It's not in me
To blubber, don't have Uncle Joe's boatload
Of whiskey in my blood yet. Heavy is how
I felt, empty-heavy and blue as poison.
So maybe it's time to quit. The green poison
Of money has leached into the ground
And turned it blue. . . That grave is mighty shallow
That I dug, but I felt so out of heart I couldn't
Make myself go farther and farther down.
I stopped waist-high and we built up a mound
That will soak away by springtime and be level."

"Are you really going to quit the farm?" I asked.
"I wouldn't quit if I could get ahead,
But busting my behind to stay behind
Has got to be the foolishest treadmill a man
Could worsen on. The farm can wait; there's money
To be made these days, and why not me?
Better me than some cheap crooks I know of,
And that's a fact."

        "Whatever you say," I said,
"It's kind of sad, though. . . And now old Honey's gone."
"*Gone?* Six nights in a row I'd close my eyes
And see her pawing up on her broken legs
Out of that blue mud, her suffering hindquarters
Still swallowed in, and in her eyes the picture
Of me coming toward her with my mattock;
And talking in a woman's pitiful voice:
Don't do it, J.T., you're breaking promises. . . .
And wake up in a sweat. Honey's not gone,
She's in my head for good and all and ever."
"Even if you quit the farm?"
                                        "Even if."

I handed him the towel. He'd washed his hands
For maybe seven minutes by the clock,
But when he gave it back there was his handprint,
Earth-colored, indelible, on the linen.

The Peaceable Kingdom of Emerald Windows

Chortlings of the green uproar of Earth,
Tree-dream, weed-dream, the man within the tree,
Woman within the weed, babies inhabit
Tea roses, at the bottom of the trumpet
Of day lily lies the yellow tabby cat,
Blackberry vine a whirlpool of green blaze,
And kudzu the Great Wall of China, oppossum
Of apple, plum tree is a sea urchin here
By the bridge of hills, crown of whitethorn bleeds
The broken sigh of hills, the hills launch here
Windows windows, summer dream is a freshet
Of windows, raindrop how much window, raindrop
An eye of glass, it is a window of
Deep sadness, it is the lover's tear of goodbye,
Goodbye I perceive to be a human creature.

Goodbye the waters of air are frisky strings.

Goodbye it is the fleeting of gorged bees.

Farewell, la Terre est veuve, farewell, goodbye.

Cheerful sixty-year-old smiling ladies,
If you could know how you sweeten my dream of stone,
You would will me all your gardens green
And send your daughters out to the shouting hayfield
With jugs of chime-clean water. The horses delicious
With sweat sang the old familiar hymns.
Down the alfalfa fell; the crickets rose,
A patent leather cloud of squeaky buttons.
I had not known that bend of river was scythe
To the other shore us gathering.
Mother and father we are distilled, the golden
Sweats of eternity surround us, heat.

The single raindrop gives us light enough
To read whole acres of Debussy, Thoreau.
And the loud hayfield diminishes to a tear,
It is the grandmother's tear of parting. Goodbye.
Amid the riotous Waterloo of hay
I think of a book open in the empty house,
It is a chapter of Psalms, and the table
Is set with tinware, Father may we go in
To dinner, the buttermilk is poured, green beans
Are fast asleep in the lukewarm oven.

O the raindrop's shape, I take its shape
To huddle, hands between my knees, in the form
The doe hare has warmed in the lespedeza,
Sweet placenta-curl, the rain is a squad
Of wet grasshoppers, me and the terrapin, us
Is asshole buddies, gaudier now in water,
What you think, bro? *Move in this wet, you crazy?*

Where rain takes its luckiest shape, the tin roof by
The rusting railroad track, where-O-where's
My tin roof sweetheart, we can get it on
On the sacks of cottonseed meal under the clatter,
No one not even the rain has such big tits,
Lend me your lip a minute, willya, lovechile?
Don't tell me I can't taste in every nook
Of flesh the hayfield wet with terrapins
And the rainsoaked cornbread and crickets and the sun,
The rainsoaked sun settles in the form
In the hay in the world in the green green hand.

The world is before the rain.

Even the downpour, Noah's deluge, is thirsty
For rain as thick as spikes, no rain is manly
Enough, we want rains of sunshot water,
Rains of quartz, rains of clover, rains
Of the blood of the curly lamb with the shepherd's staff,

Rains of semen, rains of eyes, rains
Of windows coming down like guillotines,
Windows windows raining everywhere
Their thrilling clarities of pity. Rains
Of fire.

Reach me my bumbershoot of heady ego,
I'll walk a mile or three with thee, my friend,
We'll go conversing the fields of emerald,
Reminiscing Schopenhauer, or,
If you prefer, Mozart. Pass me a light,
My matches are wet. There's some have told me, Uncle,
This world is not for real, and maybe it's so.
Are your sox as sopping as mine? An Ideal World
They say reposes in Heavenly Peas somewhere
'Midst the *Azur*, a sleepy flea market of Forms,
Kraters, amphorae, tragic destinies,
Ideas, and not a blunder in the whole blame lot.

And maybe it's so, though it sounds like a Grand Hotel
Emptied out because of chicken pox.
The Ideal World must be mighty fine,
Man wouldn't ever have to mow the lawn,
But say, Uncle Body, wouldn't our fingers starve?
Even the women there have got no luscious.

We'll walk and talk and gawk. See the flower,
Uncle, see the stone dissolving to rain
In the rain, observe the oaks. See Spot run.
Hello Dick and Jane, Uncle Body
Says you're dead, lie down with me in the form
The rabbit curled, we'll watch the world go by,
We'll look up the dresses of tan-legged women oh boy
See the mouth in the moss. See Spot run.
World-wound, come and get me, I'm dying for blood.
The goldenrod, shouldering its load of water,
Brighter than the epaulettes of Napoleon's army,
Grows stalwart at the end of sneezy summer;

Fullness of cloud, fullness of hay, erect
Strait barns, tobacco thinking of mellowing,
The hounds begin to itch for the crafty coon.
Hard sour apples are aching for my pocket,
And, Uncle Body, my teeth are longing for bitter.
Let it come down, let it all come down, summer
On its knees, and autumn fulsome as
An opera matron shall take the hill and sit there
Eating bonbons while the crickets warm
Their fiddles. Let it. Let it all go smash.
O what worms we are, ain't it the berries?

In the fields of Elysium, Uncle, we'll meet Gilbert White.
He'll have a smiling preoccupied quizzical phiz
And keep forgetting our names. Merely we want
To hear his mumble: "Woodruff blows. Martins cling
& cluster in a very particular manner.
Cucumbers come. Wheat mends . . ." Stuff like that.
I could listen all day, get drunk as a Hubbard squash.
We'll meet Linnaeus too and André Michaux
And William Bartram, Colette, rare Ben Franklin.
But it's more fun to think whom we *won't* meet.
I've got a little list, as long as the River Nile.
Am I boring you, Uncle Body?
What you want, then? A game of catch? A woman?
A corned beef sandwich obscene with Russian dressing?
All the world is lit for your delight,
Old buddy, hook it to your hulk both hands,
It's a worship of God, though kinda primitive
I admit. But then we-all is a primitive sort
Of animule.

            Help help I'm freezing to death
Here where this blizzard's lying heaped like a
Linen closet. . . Ah no, it's only a field
Of Queen Anne's Lace, no colder than a peach,
The delicate granules troubling my rib, goosing

Behind and afore as I walk snowblind to the fence.
Suppose the world went pure like this all over.
Would I be a better man? No:
Just more conspicuous. Still, in this whited
Sugar-acre I feel purified. . .
Am I an angel already? Let me lift
My wings, let me sing a salving psalm:

"I'm Popeye the sailor man!"

Reckon not. But I'll sing sweeter bye
And bye, we'll all sing like the dead men sing,
Notes as silv'ry sound as soap bubbles
From the pipe drifting out over our blue blue childhood.

I'll say this about the *Book of Earth*,
The guy who wrote it didn't cheat a jot,
Even the footnotes are brimming over with matter,
Matter aye and spirit too, each
And every page is chock to stupefying,
Any page as good as any other.
. . . Oh sure, Jean-Paul, there's a chapter on "Misery,"
And one on "Disease," a deadly dark one, "Torture,"
But tell you what, I'll trade mine for which
Ever one you choose, I'll still break even.
Bring me your tarred, your poor, your muddled asses,
I'll bear the burden on't. What I care, bo?
It's only the suffering of children that truly hurts,
Most of the others just ain't learned to read good yet.
Lemme check the Index, what'll I find,
Hemorrhoids, aw rite, fetch it hither,
I got a gut of cheerful iron, believe.
Can't be worse than reading William Buckley.

The horses thrust the breath-brown ground behind us.
Why mayn't I ride this rattletooth snagfinger
Chafeballs hayrake from here to Zanzibar?
I'll ride it flat to Heaven who'll say me Nay?

The horses are willing, been a long time ready.
Bay Maude says to Jackson: "Don't let's stop
At windrow-end, good fellow, I feel the edge
Of the world just barely beyond my hooftip,
I'm gonna make the Leap of Faith. Are you
With me?" And sober blaze-faced Jack replies:
"I'm more the pragmatist, my dear, as well
You know. It's you I've ever put my faith in.
If you consider these old bones can do it,
I'll follow you to God's dread-honey heart,
You know I will." And Maude: "I'm deeply touched,
Old lover. Maybe we'd better delay a while?
If you're feeling poorly we ought to wait until
You regain your strength, you'll enjoy it more."
"Alas, my sweet, that might in me you knew
Of old never shall return, I think.
These fields have made of me a plodding old coot;
My mind's about as sprightly as a shelf of Dreiser,
These trembling legs, everyday I curse them."
"Don't talk like that. I wasn't serious, you know.
It was just the sort of silly whim a female
Will now and then get in her head. I didn't
Actually consider going." "But you did, my love,
And now regard for me is all that keeps
You back. Go make your Leap of Faith, the grandest
Thing left in my life for me to see.
I'll urge you on with the cheerfullest hurrah.
I know you can do it." "Lacking you, I can't.
Already I'm tired. Let us just go home now."
I ride the clashbutt hayrake to the barn,
Which is heaven. Barn is home. Home is heaven.
The barn resounding like a churchbell in
The rain, *home, home, home.*

> Upshoot of crickets, butterflies, dust
> And grasshoppers precedes the tearing mower
> In the field everywhere, the visible

Ascension of a strain of Beethoven,
The hayfield birthing music, music,
A harmony of heat-breath, dark-powered
Green juices of the stalks, the blood
Of snakes and baby rabbits the mower spits
Up and out, a portable fountain
Of dear death-life, a man could
Lose a finger and a foot, lose
All thinking to watch the stalks fall neat
Like tumblers toppling off a shelf . . .
The Little Ones have lost their sky.

Our sky bulging like a sack of anthracite flowers,
Rain soon, pile that alfalfa in, rain-rot
Will heat it and eat it, keep it moving, boy,
Keep that pitchfork puffing, don't let me catch you
Heaving a pauseful sigh, we got to pitch
And poot, I'll tell you a secret, I got a bottle
Of Virgil Campbell's applejack hid behind
A joist in the hayloft, we get this in
Before the sky busts loose we'll have us a sup,
Ho there Jackson whoa-haw boy back up
Aw rite getter goin at's aw rite now whoa.

"Jack, my love, have you ever heard such idiot
Instructions in all your life?" "Never have I,
Dear Maude, these fools are half-hysterical.
Why should anyone so fear a little water?"

That blue valley between the thunderheads
Expands, contracts, like an accordion.
Our valley between the hills here flexes also
Itself like a handsome woman readying to bathe.
Ain't a blade or twig don't have its tongue out
To taste the promiseful wealthy coolskin downpour.
I'd make a Renaissance poet's wish, to be
The cloud that sluices these hills, fingering fold
And nipple, glacis and flank, cheek and crevice.

O sweet mama, I'm dying for you in gallons,
How would I ever stop, once started to come
Down? I'll rain *home* all over us.

My grandmother plants her final fork at the top.
They fling her a rope, she slides off nifty as
A schoolgirl flush with mischief. Surveys the wagon,
Satisfied? Sated, anyhow.
"Take her in, boys, I believe we'll beat the rain."
That's what we do all day, we beat the rain.

Susan's Morning Dream of Her Garden

The way a tree climbs down into the earth,
and earth to keep it from drifting like a bed
seizes the cloudmass roots;

and into ground lean the lonely
and elaborate dead as soft as sleet,
burbling one to another always,

a full Four Hundred of juicy talkers; the way
the headstrong sunflower, and boxwood, Harpwoof
Spragglewort, moondime and Dusty Miller, the pansies

with their Pekinese faces, and grimbleweed lift
out and up in light their informal forms,
pistil and petal half-shadow;

is the way my hand goes into the dirt.
Or is it flesh I enter?
My own, or lubberhubby's lying this plot with me?

Haho. He. He is loose in sleep
and musical as a horse, goeth as a zinnia
brave to daybreak and casts a watershaped snore.

Why are men so toady, tell me, touching
the moss and root? I'll tend me well my contrary garden.
Now my rows of queenly corn erupt to cadenza;

and the cabbages unfurl
outward and inward like sentences of Proust,
the sweet rose invites her oriental suitors all

iridescent in green and oil, and yonder my neat row
of bones blooms out mouths of marrow,
yet I am not replete or reconciled.

Garden, garden, will you not grow for me
a salon full of billets-doux and turtledoves?
Garden, garden, green tureen,

will you not put me forth the olden ladies upsidedown
in their hooped skirts like the bells of lilies,
their clapper legs chiming sentimental songs?

I long to belong to
the chipper elegance, those centuries where
the hand of man has never said an ugly word.

I own an antique plate in which I see
a little garden with a swing, a young girl in
the swing, tra-la, and flush with birds of every hue,

troo-loo.
The swing-girl's face is a mint of pale pink roses.
In the garden I grow I'm the girl in the swing, ting-a-ling.

And I rise and rise in my swing through the globe
of green leaves giddy till I become
a rose-pink butterfly with arms of eyes.

We whirl, my garden and I, until
the minuet boils, the sun
and moon and ground and tree become a waltzing sea,

a jiggy river of green green
green. Hurl-whorl green in which we roll _
as down a well of hay.

I sing as high and clear-O as a finch
in a yellow-green willow tree,
transparent and vivid as dragonflies.

I'd be a fool, a woman's a fool, to be drawn back
into the waking world,
all dinky clutter and dirty bathtub.

You don't catch me yet, New Day, I'm snugging

deeper in the larder of dream,
I'm burrowing like a lovely whistlepig

into the green earthflesh of sleep, keep
your tarnished-silver fingers, Sun, off my bright hair,
off my pillow, my mellow wallow.

I'm diving to a door I sense below,
a door as yellow with catlight as an owl's eye,
that opens truly into the garden

on my antique plate and can draw
my waking body in and there no one
can draw me out again. No use, you-all,

I'm gone beyond your smirch, you can't
get in, I'm the slattern in the pattern,
admire, admire!

. . . But sunlight now comes licking at my dream-door,
boohoo. *Day day go away*,
come again some other sleep.

Yet there's no help for it, and up I go
to breast the unendearing morning,
eject, usurpt, and half-awake.

I lie like cool meat on the bed like a
dimestore plate which has no picture on it,
no pattern at all.

At the Grave of Virgil Campbell

EarthMan, what o' the night? What ruinous juices
Are you fermenting here six feet under?
Never, Virgil, tell me I shan't taste them.
I leak my fervent beer on your smooth stone.

Art gone to earth, old fox? And never a dram
Shall draw thee blathering out again to light?
They've washed and laid you in a Christian plot,
Not even the thirsty widows shall claw you up,
I visit you half-smashed, you'll understand,
There's too many ragshank preachers in these hills
And not a man among them. Let's you and me
Get down, O I mean *down*, and tell some lies
To the worms and minerals. I'll tell them how
You murdered the iron bridge, you tell them sly
About Magruder's goat that wrecked the outhouse,
About the coonhound that could measure lumber,
About the flatland tourister catching the bear,
About Bad Egg that ravaged Madison County,
All that stuff . . . DeathAngel in his nightgown
Will set his candle down to listen and giggle,
All the tenants of the afterlife been saying,
"Just wait till ole Virge gets here, he's a *caution*."

I've been fumbling with some epitaphs
In case you want to try them on for size.
HERE LIES VIRGIL CAMPBELL—ONE MORE TIME.
How's that strike you? A little naked maybe.
Something a bit more classical perhaps?
      SISTE, VIATOR.
      VIRGIL CAMPBELL'S QUIET HERE.
      WHO NEVER WAS BEFORE.

Or:

    HERE'S THE FIRST TIME IT WAS SAID
    THAT VIRGIL CAMPBELL WAS GRAVELY LAID.

Or:

    EARTH, RECEIVE
    YOUR PLAYFUL LOVER
    TO HIS ONE SLEEP
    WITH NO HANGOVER.

I've got no business scribbling epitaphs
For wiser sounder men who can't hit back.
It makes me feel right sanctimonious.
So I've written one for me and here it is:

    THIS ONCE AT LEAST EARTH RAISED HER FACE
    TO ME. FOR THIS COLD KISS
    I HAVE DESERTED LOVE AND BLOOD.
    I PRAY YOU, STRANGER, PRAY ME PEACE.

Well yes *of course* it's got more dignity
Than yours, I wrote it, didn't I? . . . Howzat,
Old mole, you think it's junky-portentous?
But Virgil I'm the *poet*, had my name
In the paper once . . . Okay, here's another:

    HERE LIES FRED
    IN HIS MOSS-GROWN MANSE.
    IF HE'S NOT DEAD
    HE'S MISSING A DAMN GOOD CHANCE.

What you mean, it doesn't scan? Who's
The poet here, godammit? I write how I please.
Awright, awright, let me get a beer,
I'll write myself one last epitaph,
Don't hold your breath, though:

    OLD FRED
    HAS HAD
      IT.

There I'm through, you're through for sure, we're through
The both of us. *Salute*, I lift my Bud
Beneath the coldstone stonegray winter sky,
I drink your health for any good it'll do you,
I hope it does you oodles, it does me fine.

Here in Checkerboard City I think on bones,
The grave-rat whispers his restless runes in my ear,
The Barrow-Dwellers rise and sit on their names,
There's plenty destiny to go around
In here, I'm not worried I'll get my share.
Just look at the gleaming ghosts of them, Uncle Virgil!
Hard to picture Scruggses and Smatherses in
The gross become so lightly tenuous.
Lie down, spirits, you don't frighten me,
You left your shotguns back among the living.
But stay and tell me: the Mountains Outside Time,
Are they rife enough with coon and possum,
Have you hounds to sniff that spirit-spoor,
Do you gather round the hillside fire
And tell the tales and sip eternal moonshine?
I hope so dearly, save me a lie and a drop.
I *know* there's Whiskey-after-Death, elsewise
You wouldn't waste your time there, would you, Virgil?

You who were overmuch of earth now hold
The earth, the land beyond the dirt, unleasable
Acres of absence shining like tablecloths.
There you harvest Sundays, the long yellow
Sunday afternoons of June, you stack them
Glowing in glowing barns, eternity
Lights up like flax, like Christmas, with the hundred
Thousand billion trillion luminant Sundays.
Think of all those Sundays, Virgil, with not
A preacher in view! And the river furtive with trout,
The whistlepigs adrift in the sassafras,
The blotchy terrapins nudge the plantain,

Pasture-thistle peeps a timid purple,
Eternity at last we all go barefoot.
—This bright vision of Afterward contents me
The way a fire will sing a cat to sleep.

Here in the boneyard all the livelong day
What do you *do*? Count the rich men jamming
The needle's eye as you used to tote up Packards
On the Interstate? Count the surrealists
Trying to squeeze to Heaven through the knothole
In Grandpa's wooden leg? No you don't count,
For where you are no number is or was,
I'll bet it drives the misers crazy, I'll bet
They wish they'd never died in the first place.
I think you must spend your days playing checkers
With Moses and Jacob and the rest of the Bible crew.
Watch out King David, he's got some tricky moves,
And I've heard it said that Ananias cheats.
St. John of Patmos, don't challenge him, that guy's
Zonked out on something absolutely *weird*.
Make sure St. Peter crowns your King, of course
He will I never doubted it an instant.

Is death the cool refreshment I think it is?
Better than taking a leak? Than a fresh-cut chaw
Of Black Maria? Vivider than a dipper
Of milk lifted dripping in the springhouse
Where newt and moss cohabit red and green?
It must be so, I think I wouldn't mind
Now and then a fast cold skinnydip
In death, so long as a cramp wouldn't drag me under.
I don't want to leap for keeps, not yet
Anyhow, just want to wash the fever.
Too many drownings I've seen and had already,
There's an army of drownings been marching this earth so long
That every man among us has been stropped thin,
I'm older and newer than New will ever be,

Gimme a break, sweet Gospel, let me grow
Some skin, the sea is tired of plowing me.
The way these trees have stripped their leaves has gotta
Be right, I'll never write another novel
Full of Detail, my bones clothe over with hunger.

After last week's ice storm, Virgil, I walked
The groves in the suburbs. All the chandeliers
That ever were flew there to roost the trees,
Bare limbs decked out gaudy as matadors
Where sunlight tingled the crooked slicks and notches.
And it came to me the dead rise up in light,
We're skeletons of light we are, dimmed down
In the cloudy season of flesh. Bare bone
Bites through at last, the inner gnaws the outer,
The branches clacked like false teeth in an earthquake.
And when the ice dropped off a Tiffany's window
On the root of the tree I thought it was like a duchess
Readying for a shower, for under all
Her diamonds she's still a duchess, ain't she? You bet
Your ass she is, if you had one to bet.
Sooner or later we take St. Francis' Oath
Of Poverty, donate this human fat
To lizards and grasses, come here kitty, here's
Your bowl of Fred-meat, I hope it serves you better
Than ever it served me, I poisoned it
To sleep with alcohol, moral ideals,
And Poetry. The hard lump in your lunch?
Why that's a *bone mot*, pussycat, took me
Thirty-five ballpoint years excrescing that knot,
It must mean something. Everything means something
Even if it's Nothing, aw, stand up
Stand up with me, Virgil, we're holy trees,
Our golden boughs ope the Otherworld,
The flaming ice storms of Eternity
Shall give our bones to chatter like pissed-off squirrels,
Here's our chance to trade lies with the saints,

We'll prop our feet on the porchrail of Afterlife
And tell the seraphim about the catfish
That towed our rowboat up the waterfall,
You reckon they'll laugh and slap their thighs, the angels,
And hand around their rainbow jug of whiskey?
Indeed they will, we'll all be singing the hymns,
The good old hymns, sing Bringing in the Sheaves,
Bawl out Shall We Gather at the River?
And the one that goes:

> How teejus and tasteless the yurrs
> Till Jesus-sweet-face I do see

And all the Carter Family songs that seam
The mindstream, Hello Central Give Me Heaven
And There's a Storm Upon the Ocean, and
Jimmy Brown the Newsboy one thousand times.
But now I remember, Virgil, I've heard you sing,
There's many a man has lost his hope of heaven
For lesser crimes. Oh never mind, we'll all
Sing sweeter in the Bye-&-Bye, we'll sing
Like bristly tomcats under the sexual moon.
What good's an afterlife without our singing?
(What's whiskey without the jazz?) Pass me the bottle,
I feel one coming on, mi-mi-mi-mi,
What's this, it's not a hymn it's a drinking song,
Well, sometimes who can tell the difference?

To hell with the ragshank preachers
    Who made it out sinful to think,
And down with the dustdyed teachers
    Whose veins run Bible-black ink,
And Damn every one of those creatures
    Who told us we oughtn't to drink!
If ever they'd taken a sip
    (From me and Chris Sly
    Here's mud in their eye!)
They'd had more brains and less lip.

But here's to the happy old souls
    Who trip about clinking their chains
In time to the music that rolls
    From the locker of Davy Jones,
And here's to the Hand that controls
    Raw-Head-&-Bloody-Bones!
Let's have us a neat little nip
        (For we and the Host
        Forever cry, "Prosit!")
Before we take our last sleep.

Let's put on our nightcaps of moonshine
    And kneel and mumble our prayers,
In Glory we drunkards will soon shine
    Singing our spiritous airs,
And, tipsy as possums by noontime,
    We'll roll down Pisgah like bears!
So pour us a tight little drop
        (And here's to the Splendor
        Of the Holy Bartender!)
And we're ready at last for our nap.

How to Build the Earthly Paradise:
Letter to George Garrett

> Io vidi già nel comminciar del giorno
> la parte oriental tutta rosata
> e l'altro ciel di bel sereno adorno.
> —*Purgatorio*, XXX.

Stone,
    quarried
out of the wistful starpaths,
stone first of all deep sunk into
the toiled-up footing, stone from space,
where the walls dig in their roots and bind
force over force in steady fabric
    rising
        up.

Sand
    next, strewn
white and golden on the hewed-out
stone and somewhat muffling its hunger,
the sand inviting as a table-
cloth, "here spread your quaint paradise,
your long pink carnival of sweetmeats,"
    shining
        soft.

Earth,
    acres
of worm-meal earth over sand and stone,
a dirt so rich our warm rude fingers
tingle inside it, rubbing the plasma
ancestral, rye-flour loam which takes

the signature of hoe and plow,
            sleeping
                    long.

        Dead
            people
in earthwrack, in the layered gritcake,
let us gently allay them, the dead
are troublous in their cool sleep, they stir
and grumble, blind wall of hands
beneath, blind well-mouths upthrust,
            water-
                    speech.

        Then
            water,
waters forcible in dirt
and flesh, their tendons streak the air,
rounded waters widely vying
the built-in skies, waters that mutter
the double names inside the earth,
            sweep clouds
                    through.

        Air
            where light
is and where light is not, it holds the
light the way a hand holds water, and
the dark it holds, air alive as
minnows, windheap, the checkered music
light/dark   light/dark, vision stands
            forth in
                    air.

        Green
            plants for
the heart's delectation, the rough-red
singing vine glows with fire-oils, the

willful grasses, daisies gleaming like
turnip watches, slime-mold, orchid,
tiger lilies snapping fence links, the
                    modest
                         fern.

                    The
                    sleeping
and unsleeping animals, alert
with breath and licking the unaddled impulse
that sustains the bones, furred shaggy
or smooth in land or ocean, animals
that make their nests in grass, their
                    skins are
                         eyes.

                    What,
                    Giorgio,
have we omitted? *Men and women
and children?* Let's by all means
have them, by the century and the multitude,
we need some middle-muddle here to keep
the sky from being so polar-miserable
                    lonesome
                         cold.

                    That's
                    how I'd
build it, the Earthly Paradise: no
different, how could it be?, from what
it was ever dreamed, harsh floodtide
of feathervein delight each instant at
every hand, the troubador atoms
                    dancing
                         full.

                    Is
                    it true

already, what if it's true already? and
we have but to touch out to see it
among our amidst, how then can we say
ourselves guiltless ever, not partaking,
forswearing the joyous hale, we ought
            to be
                  shot.

                  No
            more, I
never no more will turn my back
upon, cast down my eyes away from,
that spinning spanning spuming spawning
shoal of burnished juices, the seething
homebrew of creation creating, I swear it
            in my
                  bones.

                  New
            now you
see me a new man, unshucked from
my soiled hide, I'm coming belchlike out of
the cave, make way my friends make way,
here gleaming with unspotted dream, here
clamorous with tincture, is yes your
            old friend
                  Fred.

My Grandmother's Dream of Plowing

I never saw him plowing, but Frank was well
And whole and plowing in the field behind
Jackson and Maude whose heads went up and down
Like they agreed on what they were talking over.
There was a light around him, light he was blind
To, light tolling steady like a bell.
The dirt peeled back from the share like meal, brown
Loam all water-smelling. What he'd uncover
With his plowing I felt I already knew:
He'd turn up that bell from the church the Klan
Burned down because of the Negro organist.
The bell they couldn't find had washed in the tide
Of earth and finally had come to rest
In our own bottom land that used to grow
Tobacco . . .
              I was wrong; for when the sun
Gleamed on something in the furrow-side
I went to look, and it wasn't a bell at all.
It was a big and shining lump of gold.
It was a Mystery gold, and just the tip
Of it stuck out. With my bare hands I brushed
Away the crumbs and dug it out of the soil.
I got on my knees and tried to wrestle it up,
And after a while I did, aching, and rolled
It out and stood looking at it all hushed.
About as big as a twenty-five-pound sack
Of flour. And burning burning like the flame
Of Moses' bush. It lay there in the furrow
Like, like . . . Oh, I can't say what like.
I picked it up and cradled it to my breast,
Thinking how this was a Gold made out of dream

And now we'd never fear about tomorrow
And give our frets and cares a well-earned rest.

"Is that your baby that was never mine?"
Behind me Frank had stopped the plow. His voice
Came up against me like another person,
Like a stranger maybe intending harm.
His voice was dressed in black and laid a curse on
All the fancies I'd thought up for us.
I turned around to tell him Hush, but then
I knew it *was* a baby in my arm,
The strangest baby. As fat and dimpled as
The Baby Jesus in the pictures on
The Upper Room. And this golden child was
Speaking to me, not just baby-talk,
But real words that I ought to understand.
Except I couldn't hear. Bent my head down
But couldn't hear, no more than you hear the dark.
"It's not my baby, and just never you mind,"
I said to Frank. "This baby I've found will bring
Us luck," I said, "because it turned from gold
To flesh. That means—it has to mean—something
To us, something to help us when we're old."
"We're old," Frank said, "we're old already, Anne.
And, see, the baby's changed to something else.
It's turned into an ugly little man."
I looked, and felt the beating of my pulse
Grow harder in my throat, knowing it was true.

I held to me an evil little goblin
With an evil smile. And, must-be, astray in its mind,
The way its eyes were loose, and its head bobbling
Up and down like corn tassel in the wind.
All over I went water then and trembled
Like a flame of fire. I turned my face away
From Frank. I'd never felt so ashen-humbled.

What had I brought upon us? *Oh what, what?*

Something terrible the field had birthed,
And now I'd gathered it up, and who could say
It wouldn't haunt us forever from this day
Onward? I'd never thought such ugly thought
As standing there with what the plow unearthed
And wishing it would go away. Or die.
That's what I wished: *Please die, and let us be.*

Now here's the awfullest part. What I said
To do, it did. It rolled its eyes glass-white
Back in its head, and kicked and shivered like
A new-born calf, and murmured in white froth
A tiny whimper, and opened on its mouth
A glassy bubble and sucked it gagging back
Into its throat, and opened and closed its throat,
And sighed a sigh, and lay in my arms stone dead.

It was my fault. It turned into a stone,
And it was all my fault, wishing that way.
Whatever harm had the little goblin done?
And now I'd killed it. I began to cry,
And cried so hard I felt my eyes dissolve
To dust, to water, fire, and then to smoke.

"And then you woke," I said, "to the world you love."

"And now I know," she said, "I never woke."

My Grandfather Dishes the Dirt

Who is walking on my grave?
Is it my Family up there come to bring
Me flowers, come to have

A latter word or two? It must be Spring,
That's when you always come . . .
When every juice is flourishing,

Have you no better chore than standing about my tomb?
Please understand, I *like* it here,
Dreaming in cold earth my freshened dream.

It's true the things I left behind are dear
To me, and maybe in some ways
Now dearer. The turning of the year

Sweetly I remember, and blue May days
Leap out in my grave sleep
Like sun-drunk butterflies.

But mostly now I keep
My thoughts as cool and quiet as the stare
Of glinting spring water in a tin cup.

I wish that I could share
With you—. . . But no, of course I can't . . .
You know already as you require.

The knowing that now I know would daunt
Your spirits,
Sickly them over with the pale cast of want.

Death disinherits
Us of wanting, I find.
Here where it's

Still not Absolute I'm lying blind
To itch and wish
And still am not resigned.

To tell the truth, I'm devilish
Hard put to it to think
Of anything much to say which

Now you'd care to hear. It's dark as ink
Down here, and kind of lonely,
And as mysterious as a wink;

But you don't want to hear all that. Only
Always my thoughts reach out
To silence, to a stonily

Determined silence, broken by a shout
Now and then of starburst,
Or a glittering rout

Of softly spilling dust.
What's that to you,
Still toiling luck and work and lust?

The dead I'm here to say have nothing to say.
Our job is merely to listen and look
From now until the Judgment Day

When we can see once more in the Judgment Book
All that we've seen already, each nook
And cranny of us forever on display.

Let's let each other alone, for Jesus' sake.

Stillpoint Hill That Other Shore

This ground, Susan, is full of hands,
hands filled with earth,
voices of the hands of earth,
the finger-tendrils of earthroots
stroke our bones, this is the hill
at midnight,
the moon devours
bones out of the ground, the moon
signs the firmament
in the steady hand
of the faithful dead. We can read
at last the firepoint
constellations all in the deep
where the other earths are swimming.
The stars see us
with new eyes.

Restored to earth, returned
from earth, our hands
and voices interlace
like the fires of double suns.
Do we see each other,
one another in unsteady
starshine?
Do I unsteady not see
you steady?

This hill above our house,
stillpoint before
the turning begins again,
earth solid to the hand,
earth moveless in time,

comprised
of the husk and marrow of
our dead forefathers.
Unmoving in time,
only the dead are incorrupt.

Time I shall not serve thee.
You Earth I have loved most blest.

Our futures in the dirt
speak to us, saying,
The Old Unmoved is a-movering,
have you yet prepared
your spirit for the starry waters?
I have not I am not,
Earth,
prepared, here let me rest
unready, Susan has taken my hand,
we step forward blind
into the blind windcurrent of the soil.
The murders and betrayals,
wounds, firefevers, bloodtwitchings,
the burning suicides, the tortured genitals,
the vacant children,
ruin of seed, mind-ruin, sleep-ruin,
nightmare of the sickened animals,
hold these in peace away from us
for this moment.
We beaten creatures cannot evermore
bear. Too long
we have thrashed in earthfire,
our limbs quiver,
exhaustion of stale guilt.

Susan has taken my hand, I clutch
her voice though it comes fitful
in the starshot earthdark.
Her voice is in surges
the soothing of a thousand waters.

In veins of my sleep
I feel the piling of those waters,
cool mouths mirroring dark sky
where no words shine, where
the Tree of Spirit lifts its roots
among the black stars whirling
collapsed to nervous cinder.
These are the flower-worlds with all
the visionary petals shriveled away.

Please hold my hand, may we
go down now, home?
Where booklight and kitchen light
furrow the silence?
In the dark, two lights,
like two strokes of a churchbell,
home, home.
Can you not hear it tolling,
our toothsome sleep we may at last attain?
It calls to me, calls,
and my whole blood
is avid for that earth,
that sleep.

Sleeping we are harmless at last.
Through silence moves a cloudless peace.

The peace that shall seize us
in sleepgrip,
that peace shall I tell you
be all the black frenzies of our flesh
in one green cuddle,
let us descend to our house
our bed
and invite the mornings,
the infinite anniversary mornings,
which reach out to touch us
with the hands of one another.

Earthsleep

It is the bottomless swoon of never forgetting.

It is the foul well of salvation.

It is the skin of eternity like a coverlet.

It is a tree of fire with tongues of wind.

It is the grandfather lying in earth and the father digging,
The mother aloft in air, the grandmother sighing.

It is the fire that eats the tree of fire.

It is Susan in the hand of sleep a new creature.

I am a new creature born thirty-five years to this earth
Of jarring elements, its fractuous hold
On the man and woman brings
Earth to bloodmouth.
                Here where I find
I am I founder.
            Lord Lord
Let this lost dark not.

Who's used?
Who's not scrawled upon
By the wilderness hand of
Earth and fire and water and air?

How simple simple blessèd simple.

It is the fathomless noon that blossoms after midnight,
And daybreak at the margin of the oaks
Begins to sculpt our sleeping bodies
In the wimpled bed.

What shapes may we take now
Where destiny uncurls its roots of fire?

Let it then be flesh that we take on
That I may see you
Cool in time and blonde as this fresh daybreak.

No one no one sleeps apart
Or rises separate
In the burning river of this morning
That earth and wind overtake.

The way the light rubs upon this planet
So do I press to you,

Susan   Susan

The love that moves the sun and other stars
The love that moves itself in light to loving
Flames up like dew

Here in the earliest morning of the world.

Sir Toby. A false conclusion: I hate it as an unfilled can. To be up after midnight and to go to bed then, is early; so that to go to bed after midnight is to go to bed betimes. Does not our life consist of the four elements?

Sir Andrew. Faith, so they say; but I think it rather consists of eating and drinking.

Sir Toby. Thou art a scholar; let us therefore eat and drink. Marian, I say! a stoup of wine!

—*Twelfth Night*